THE EMANCIPATION PROCLAMATION

Dallas Public Library

BY SETH LYNCH

Gareth Stevens
PUBLISHING

CRASHCOURSE

Please visit our website, www.garethstevens.com. For a free color catalog of all our high-quality books, call toll free 1-800-542-2595 or fax 1-877-542-2596.

Library of Congress Cataloging-in-Publication Data

Names: Lynch, Seth, author.
Title: The Emancipation Proclamation / Seth Lynch.
Description: New York : Gareth Stevens Publishing, 2019. | Series: A look at US history | Includes index.
Identifiers: LCCN 2017040520| ISBN 9781538221198 (library bound) | ISBN 9781538221211 (pbk.) | ISBN 9781538221228 (6 pack)
Subjects: LCSH: United States. President (1861-1865 : Lincoln). Emancipation Proclamation--Juvenile literature. | Lincoln, Abraham, 1809-1865--Juvenile literature. | Slaves--Emancipation--United States--Juvenile literature. | United States--Politics and government--1861-1865--Juvenile literature.
Classification: LCC E453 .L96 2018 | DDC 973.7092--dc23
LC record available at https://lccn.loc.gov/2017040520

First Edition

Published in 2019 by
Gareth Stevens Publishing
111 East 14th Street, Suite 349
New York, NY 10003

Designer: Samantha DeMartin
Editor: Kristen Nelson

Photo credits: Series art Christophe BOISSON/Shutterstock.com; (feather quill) Galushko Sergey/Shutterstock.com; (parchment) mollicart-design/Shutterstock.com; cover, p. 1 SuperStock/SuperStock/Getty Images; pp. 5, 9 PSboom/Shutterstock.com; p. 7 Everett Historical/Shutterstock.com; p. 11 UniversalImagesGroup/Universal Images Group/ Getty Images; pp. 13, 15 courtesy of the Library of Congress; p. 17 Ed Vebell/Archive Photos/ Getty Images; p. 19 GraphicaArtis/Archive Photos/Getty Images; p. 21 Clindberg/Wikimedia Commons; p. 23 Kean Collection/Archive Photos/Getty Images; p. 25 Gamaliel/Wikimedia Commons; p. 27 Photo 12/Universal Images Group/Getty Images; p. 29 Muddymari/ Shutterstock.com.

Printed in the United States of America

CPSIA compliance information: Batch #CS18GS: For further information contact Gareth Stevens, New York, New York at 1-800-542-2595.

CONTENTS

Words in the glossary appear in **bold** type the first time they are used in the text.

THE STATE OF THE UNION

By the mid-1800s, **tension** existed between the North, which had mostly outlawed slavery, and the South, which depended on slavery as part of their economy. A group of Southern states **threatened** to secede, or break away, if the antislavery Republican Party won the 1860 presidential election.

The United States in 1860

Washington Territory
OR
Nebraska Territory
Unorganized Territory
MN
WI
VT
ME
NH
MA
RI
CT
NY
MI
IA
PA
Utah Territory
IL
IN
OH
NJ
DE
MD
CA
Kansas Territory
MO
KY
VA
New Mexico Territory
Indian Territory
AR
TN
NC
SC
MS
AL
GA
TX
LA
FL

SLAVE STATES

FREE STATES

TERRITORIES OPEN TO SLAVERY

MAKE THE GRADE

When some states joined the United States during the 1800s, they were allowed to choose whether they would allow slavery.

SECESSION

Abraham Lincoln was the Republican candidate—and he won. By the time he took office on March 4, 1861, seven states had seceded. This would increase to 11 states total, which came together to form the Confederate States of America.

The fighting in the American Civil War began on April 12, 1861.
That's when Confederate soldiers fired on Union, or Northern,
troops at Fort Sumter in Charleston, South Carolina.

7

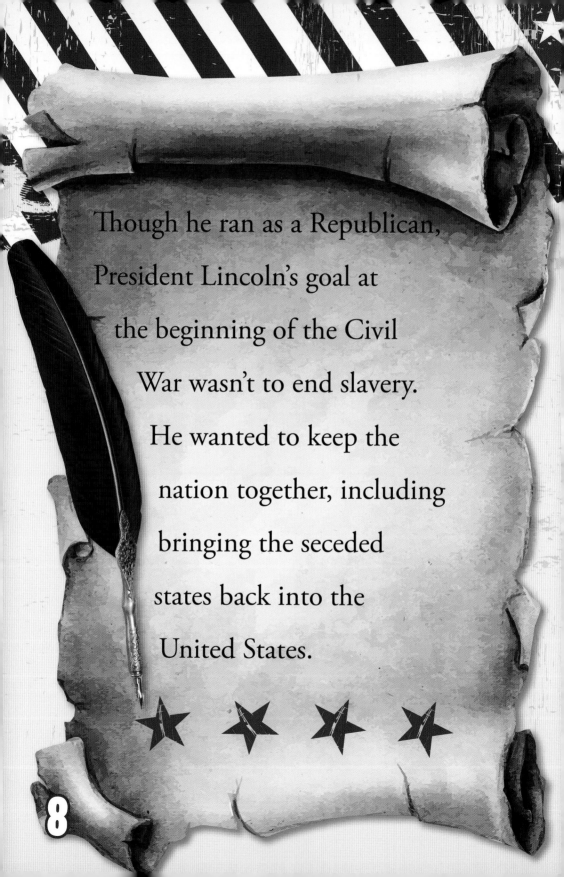

Though he ran as a Republican, President Lincoln's goal at the beginning of the Civil War wasn't to end slavery. He wanted to keep the nation together, including bringing the seceded states back into the United States.

MAKE THE GRADE

Some slave states didn't secede, including Missouri,
Kentucky, Maryland, Delaware, and later West Virginia.
Lincoln didn't want to lose these border states,
as they were called, by outright outlawing slavery.

FREE STATES

slave states seceded:

BEFORE WAR BROKE OUT

AFTER WAR BROKE OUT

BORDER STATES (AND WEST VIRGINIA)

UNION-HELD TERRITORIES

CONGRESS ACTS

Congress wanted to take action against slavery, though. It passed the first Confiscation Act in August 1861. This act said the Union could take, or confiscate, property belonging to Confederates. It freed slaves working or fighting for the Confederate army, too.

In July 1862, the second Confiscation Act was passed. It said slaves of all Confederate officials were free, though Union troops could only enforce it when they were in an area.

A PRELIMINARY PROCLAMATION

Congress's passage of the Confiscation Acts made Lincoln feel like he had enough support to take a stand on slavery. He wrote what's now called the **preliminary** Emancipation Proclamation in July 1862. This **document** was **issued** on September 22, 1862.

MAKE THE GRADE

Upon hearing the preliminary proclamation,
Lincoln's **cabinet** was uneasy.

13

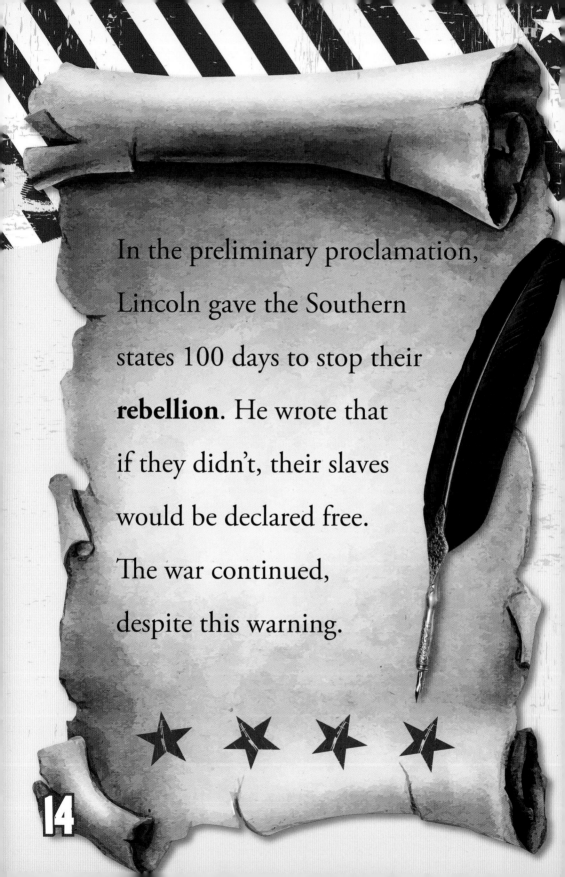

In the preliminary proclamation, Lincoln gave the Southern states 100 days to stop their **rebellion**. He wrote that if they didn't, their slaves would be declared free. The war continued, despite this warning.

MAKE THE GRADE

The preliminary proclamation was issued right after the
Union won the Battle of Antietam.

NEW YEAR'S PROCLAMATION

True to his word, President Lincoln issued the final Emancipation Proclamation on January 1, 1863. Before he signed it, Lincoln said, "I never, in my life, felt more certain that I was doing right than I do in signing this paper."

MAKE THE GRADE

Lincoln didn't call a cabinet meeting or hold a **ceremony** when he signed the proclamation. Only a few friends saw him sign it at the White House.

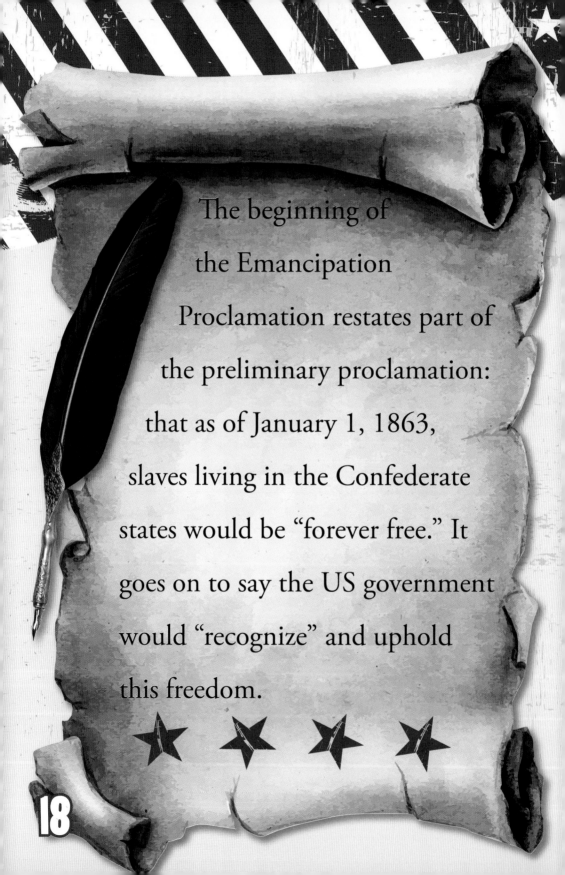

The beginning of the Emancipation Proclamation restates part of the preliminary proclamation: that as of January 1, 1863, slaves living in the Confederate states would be "forever free." It goes on to say the US government would "recognize" and uphold this freedom.

FREEDOM FOR ALL, BOTH BLACK AND WHITE!

PROCLAMATION OF EMANCIPATION

MAKE THE GRADE

Some people in the Northern states didn't think the Emancipation Proclamation went far enough to end slavery in the United States.

Lincoln asks in the proclamation for those who have been set free not to fight unless they have to **defend** themselves. It's likely he wanted to support a peaceful **transition**, since there was already a terrible war going on.

vernment of the United States, including

he military and naval authorities thereof,

ill recognize and maintain the freedom of said

ersons.

And I hereby enjoin upon the people so

declared to be free to abstain from all violence,

unless in necessary self-defence; and I recom-

mend to them that, in all cases when allowed,

hey labor faithfully for reasonable wages.

And I further declare and make known,

hat such persons of suitable condition, will

e received into the armed service of the United

tates to garrison forts, positions, stations, and

ther places, and to man vessels of all sorts in

aid service.

And upon this act, sincerely believed to be

n act of justice, warranted by the Constitution,

pon military necessity, I invoke the consider-

te judgment of mankind, and the gracious

Lincoln wrote that the freed slaves should go to
work for pay where they could.

tates to be affixed.

The Emancipation Proclamation also says that freed slaves who are able would be welcomed into the Union forces to fight the Confederate army. This was an important addition.

As the fighting went on, more and more men were needed on both sides of the war.

MAKE THE GRADE

Before the end of the war, close to 200,000 black men fought for the Union.

THE EXCEPTIONS

The Emancipation Proclamation
made clear that it ended slavery
for the Confederate states.
However, it also clearly did
not end slavery in the border
states. Parts of Louisiana
and the parts of Virginia
that became West Virginia
were written exceptions to
the proclamation.

MAKE THE GRADE

Lincoln didn't feel he had the power to outlaw slavery completely. Congress would need to pass a law.

RIGHTS FOR ALL?

Slavery in the United States didn't end with the Emancipation Proclamation. However, it did start the country on the road to end it. After the war finally ended in 1865, the Thirteenth **Amendment** passed. It outlawed, or abolished, slavery in all of the United States.

MAKE THE GRADE

President Lincoln didn't see the end of the war in
June 1865 or the passage of the Thirteenth Amendment
in December 1865. He was shot on April 14, 1865,
and died the next day.

27

The Emancipation Proclamation was one of the most important documents of its day. Lincoln's bold move to end slavery in the Confederate states is one of the most honored parts of his presidency. This proclamation was a small step toward granting everyone equal rights.

MAKE THE GRADE

The Fourteenth Amendment made all freed slaves
citizens of the United States.

IN THIS TEMPLE
AS IN THE HEARTS OF THE PEOPLE
FOR WHOM HE SAVED THE UNION
THE MEMORY OF ABRAHAM LINCOLN
IS ENSHRINED FOREVER

TIMELINE OF THE EMANCIPATION PROCLAMATION

November 1860

Abraham Lincoln is elected president.

December 20, 1860

South Carolina is the first state to secede from the Union.

March 4, 1861

President Lincoln takes office.

April 12, 1861

Shots are fired at Fort Sumter, starting the American Civil War.

August 6, 1861

Congress passes the first Confiscation Act.

July 17, 1862

Congress passes the second Confiscation Act.

September 22, 1862

Lincoln issues the preliminary Emancipation Proclamation.

January 1, 1863

Lincoln issues the Emancipation Proclamation.

December 6, 1865

The Thirteenth Amendment outlaws slavery.

August 20, 1866

President Johnson formally declares an end to the war.

GLOSSARY

amendment: a change or addition to a constitution

cabinet: heads of government departments who are appointed by the president and act as special advisors

ceremony: an event to honor or celebrate something

defend: to guard against harm

document: a formal piece of writing

issue: to put forth

preliminary: something that comes before a main document or work

rebellion: a fight to overthrow a government

tension: a state of anger between groups

threaten: to announce as possible

transition: a change from one state to another

FOR MORE INFORMATION

Books

Cummings, Judy Dodge. *The Emancipation Proclamation.* Minneapolis, MN: Essential Library, 2017.

Otfinoski, Steven. *The Civil War.* New York, NY: Scholastic, 2017.

Website

The Emancipation Proclamation
www.archives.gov/exhibits/featured-documents/emancipation-proclamation
See the National Archives online exhibit of the Emancipation Proclamation.

INDEX